THE CLAYTON FAMILY

THE CLAYTON FAMILY

BY

HENRY F. HEPBURN

GYAN

ISBN : 978-81-212-1773-6 (PB)

First Published, 1904

Published, 2018

Published by

Gyan Publishing House
5, Ansari Road
Daryaganj, New Delhi-110002
Phone: 011-47034999, 9811692060
www.gyanbooks.com
E-mail: books@gyanbooks.com

Printed at: G. Print Process, Delhi.

THE CLAYTON FAMILY.

It is well to start with the family history at the foundation, and then follow it up through its various changes to the present time. We will start about 912, when Rollo made peace with the King of France, and the Dukedom of Normandy was confirmed. In that settlement after a thirty years war, the King of France agreed to confirm Rollo's title as Duke of Normandy, and give him his daughter in marriage; the Duke agreeing to do homage to the King, to become a Christian and marry the King's daughter. But when the time came for the Duke to do homage, he refused to kiss the King's foot, and no persuasion or entreaty could induce him to perform that part of the ceremony. It was finally compromised by permitting Rollo to kiss the King's foot by proxy, but when the courtier lifted up the King's foot, he raised it so high that it tumbled the King out of his chair, which created great laughter among those present. Yet the King bore this indignity, well knowing that Rollo's army was too strong to meet in battle.

From that time Normandy began to flourish, and during the time of its first six dukes, it was one of the richest provinces in the world, notwithstanding its many wars. When "William the Conqueror", who was the seventh Duke, came upon the stage of action, Normandy was divided into two classes, the nobility, who were the descendants of Rollo's followers, and the peasants who were the descendants of the French; so that we find a class of cultured people, who had much of the polish of Paris, and who were far in advance of the Saxons in England.

During the time of the quarrel between William the Conqueror and King Harold, William called together his chieftains in council. Some were willing to go to war while others refused; but one of his brainy men "Fitzosborne" advised the Duke to call upon the nobility separately, which was done, and in a short time sufficient men and means were ready for his enterprise. A man by the name of Robert, born in Caudebec Normandy, France, accompanied William the Conqueror to England. He was a soldier well skilled in arms, and after the battle of Hastings, had the Manor of Clayton given him by William the Conqueror for his laudable services in battle. He was afterwards known as "Robert de Clayton" and was Lord of the Manor of Clayton, and the first Clayton spoken of in the history of England.

He had three sons:—John, William and Robert. John accompanied William Rufus in his war against "Malcolm" King of Scotland, and fell nobly in battle near Penrith, in Cumberland. William de Clayton, the second son, succeeded his father. He faithfully served King Stephen in all his troubles, and on Candlemas Day, 1141, he lost his life in battle, and was succeeded by his son Robert.

Robert had one son William de Clayton. He married Elizabeth Farrington, of Farrington. He had three sons and died in 1152 and was buried at Leyland, Lancashire. The eldest son, Richard, was a priest of a very benevolent character and died in Normandy. Thomas, the second son, died without issue and Robert de Clayton, the third son, succeeded his father. He married in 1151 and had four

JOHN M. CLAYTON.

sons:—William, Robert, John and Thomas. Three of the sons accompanied King John into Normandy in 1200 and died without issue. John the third son succeeded his father. He had two sons William and Thomas and died in 1209 and was succeeded by his second son Thomas de Clayton.

Thomas de Clayton had three sons, John, Robert and William. John, the eldest son, succeeded his father. He married in 1263 and died in 1280, having had issue two sons, Thomas and Ralph. He was succeeded by his second son Ralph de Clayton who left three sons, John, Giles and Nicholas, and he was succeeded by his eldest son, John de Clayton. This John accompanied John of Gaunt in 1356 to assist the King of Navarre against the French. He also accompanied King Edward in most of his expeditions. He left four sons: John, William, Ralph and Robert and died in 1399 and was succeeded by his eldest son John de Clayton, who had three sons, Thomas, Robert and William, he died in 1404, and was buried at Leyland, and was succeeded by his eldest son. Thomas de Clayton married Dorothy Thellwell of Thellwell in Cheshire with whom he received that township and village as a marriage portion and by whom he had two sons, John born in 1419, and William born in 1420. (William died without issue in 1471.) Thomas de Clayton died in 1426 and was succeeded by his eldest son, John de Clayton, who married, in 1440, Mary Mainwaring.

ANCESTRY OF MARY MAINWARING.

The Mainwarings are the descendants of "Ranulphus, one of the companions of William the Conqueror in the Norman Invasion and also one of those thirty-two persons, to whom that fortunate monarch gave all or most of Cheshire, of which he obtained fifteen lordships in Peure (now Overpever) which remained in the family until 1700."

His grandson, Roger, had a son named William, who was the father of Sir Ralph Mainwaring, Knt., who was a Judge of Chester in the reign of Richard (1). He is the first Mainwaring spoken of in history. He married Amicia, daughter of Hugh Kyviliok, Earl of Chester, whose ancestors were as follows:—

After the conquest, William the Conqueror, gave to his nephew, Hugh Lupus, the Earldom of Chester about the year 1070. He died July 27, 1101, leaving a son, his heir.

II. Richard, second Earl of Chester who married but died without issue, and the Earldom descended to the nephew of Hugh Lupus by his sister Maude.

III. Randal (1) Earl of Chester. He was Randall Meschines, V. C., of Bayeaux, Normandy, France, and married Lucy, a daughter of Algar, the Saxon Earl of Marcia and died 1128, leaving issue his son and heir.

IV. Randal (2) Earl of Chester, who became a great warrior and took King Stephen prisoner. He married Maude, daughter of Robert, Earl of Gloucester, a natural son of King Henry (1) of England and died 1153 leaving two sons, Hugh and Richard and was succeeded by his eldest son.

V. Hugh (2) Earl of Chester. He married Bertred, a daughter of Simon, Earl of Evereaux, Normandy, France, by whom he had (1) Randal, (2) Maude, who married David, Earl of Huntingdon, and was a brother of William, King of Scotland, (3) Mabil, who married William .... Albiny, Earl of Arundel, (4) Agnes, who married William Ferrars, Earl of Derby, (5) Hawaise, who married Robert Quincy, son and heir of Sabil de Quincy, Earl of Winchester.

He had another daughter not of this marriage named Amacia (Amice) over whom a great controversy was carried on between Sir Peter Leycester and Sir Thomas Mainwaring, Sir Peter claiming that she was an illegitimate daughter and Sir Thomas claiming that she was a legitimate daughter. Finally the question was referred to the Judges of Chester, who decided that Amacia was the legitimate daughter of Hugh (5) Earl of Chester and the heralds quartered the arms of the Earls of Chester with the Mainwarings. Amacia married Rause (Ralph) Mainwaring and it appears from the manuscripts that Bertred, the wife of Hugh Cyviliok, second, (5) Earl of Chester, witnessed a deed in frank marriage with said Amacia. By this marriage there were two children, one of whom, the daughter, was named after Bertred, the Countess of Chester, and a son named Randal, who became the head of the Mainwaring Family of Over-pever in Cheshire about 1175, and from whom the Mainwaring Family descended.

It will thus appear that this Amacia Mainwaring had in her the blood of William the Conqueror and the old Saxon Earls. She was the great grand-daughter of Henry (1) King of England, and great grand-daughter of the Earl

Garva of Marcia, also a descendant of the Earls of Normandy, and the early Saxon Kings.

Her half sister Maude was the ancestor of Baloil, King of Scotland, also of Robert Bruce, King of Scotland and his descendants, making her related to the ancient Anglo-Saxon Kings, to the English Norman Kings, to the Scotch Kings, and the nobility of Normandy.

Robert Fitzroy, her grand-father, was a scholar and a soldier, and commanded the forces of Empress Maude against King Stephen. From the above recital it clearly shows that Mary Mainwaring who married John de Clayton was a lineal descendant of Hugh Cyviliok, Earl of Chester through his daughter Amacia, who married Ralph Mainwaring. The Mainwaring family is very old, and the founder Ranulf received fifteen manors or lordships in Cheshire for his services to William the Conqueror.

John de Clayton, who married Mary Mainwaring of Cheshire, had by her two sons, first: Thomas, who was afterwards disinherited for disobeying his parents, (2) William and also three daughters. His first wife died in 1445 and he married secondly Jane Clifton, by whom he had two sons Robert and Richard. Robert the eldest son, by the second wife, died in Paris in 1471 without issue, and Richard Clayton, the youngest son by the second wife succeeded to the estate, but dying without issue, he was succeeded by William de Clayton, a son of Thomas de Clayton and he dying without issue was succeeded by Robert Clayton, third son of Thomas who was disinherited. Robert Clayton as above, married Jane Farrington, by whom he had four sons:—Thomas, born in 1498; John born in 1499; Edward born in 1505; and Richard born in 1506, and

SARAH (MIDDLETON) CLAYTON,
THE MOTHER OF JOHN M. CLAYTON.

three daughters. He died 1510 and was buried at Leyland and was succeeded by his eldest son Thomas Clayton who married, in 1561-3, Anne Jackson, of Bocking in Essex, and had two sons, Robert and William, and died in 1580. Robert, the eldest son, was of St. John's College and Vice-Chancellor of Cambridge. He married and had one son, John Clayton. This John Clayton had a son, Richard, and two daughters, Dorothy and Elizabeth.

He died December 20, 1623, aged twenty-seven years and was succeeded by Richard Clayton, his eldest and only son, who died by a fall from his horse, without issue.

The family estates of Clayton and Crook went by virtue of the settlement to Dorothy, his eldest sister, who was the wife of George Leycester, of Toft in Cheshire, Esquire. Whereupon the Lordship of Clayton, granted by William the Conqueror, went with this Dorothy Clayton, to her husband, and was afterward sold. This must have occurred about 1650 or 1660.

The line was continued by William Clayton, second son of Thomas Clayton and Anne Jackson. He had five sons (1) Thomas, born in 1585, (2) William, born in 1587, (3) John, born in 1588, (4) Ralph, born in 1589, (5) Richard, born in 1592 and was succeeded by his eldest son, Thomas Clayton, who had the estates in Fulwood in Lancashire settled upon him and his issue.

He married and had issue: Robert; Thomas, born in 1630 and one daughter, Annie. Robert had four sons: Thomas, William, John and Richard. Thomas, the eldest son, had one son, Robert, born 1695, who became the Bishop of Clogher, and died Feb. 26, 1756. He bequeathed his Lancashire estate to his nearest male heir "The Right

Honorable Richard Clayton, Lord Chief Justice of The Common Pleas in Ireland.'' Thomas Clayton, the second son of Thomas, on the death of the Bishop, became the representative of the family. He married a daughter of John Atherton by whom he had five sons: (1) Thomas, (2) John, (3) Richard, (4) Thomas, of whom hereafter, (5) Robert and seven daughters. This Thomas purchased the Lordships and estates of Worthington and Adlington and died in the ninety-second year of his age. Thomas, the eldest son of Thomas Clayton and Ann Atherton, married in 1697, Martha, daughter of Joshua Horton, of Chaderton, Esq., by whom he had five sons: Thomas, William, Richard, Edward and John and four daughters. He died in 1728 at Adlington in the sixty-first year of his age. Thomas, his eldest son, died in 1735 unmarried.

Richard, the third son, was brought up to the bar and became King's counsel, and afterwards Lord Chief Justice of the Common Pleas in Ireland, which office he resigned in 1774, and died the same year aged sixty-eight. By his will dated the sixteenth day of March, 1772, he devised his Manors of Adlington and Worthington to his nephew, Richard Clayton.

The successor in line was John Clayton, the fifth son. He had four sons: Richard, Robert, William and John, and was succeeded by his eldest son, Richard Clayton, Esq., who was admitted to the Inner Temple in 1762, called 1771, and made a reader in 1811. He was created a baronet May 3, 1774, and died in 1828. This ancient family produced soldiers of valor and skill, preachers and monks of great learning, and lawyers and jurists of great ability.

We will now take up the family in Yorkshire, a branch of the family of "The Manor of Clayton."

As it is well known that from 1500 to 1660 the History of England met with so many disasters, it is next to impossible to get the family registry of the various branches during that period.

We find in 1499 that Robert Clayton of the Manor of Clayton had a son born named John. It is contended that this John settled in Yorkshire and was the founder of Clayton Hall. His eldest brother, Thomas, succeeded to the Manor of Clayton, but did not marry until he was over sixty years old. John married and had two sons, Thomas, his heir, and Richard of Wakefield, Yorkshire. The names that follow are similar to the names of the family of the Manor of Clayton, the dates harmonize, but the strongest evidence of the relationship is the arms borne by the family.

The arms of the descendants of the Manor of Clayton of Lancashire and the arms of the descendants of John Clayton of Clayton Hall are the same. It is claimed that John Clayton, second son of Robert Clayton, and great grandson of John de Clayton and Mary Mainwaring, was the founder of Clayton Hall, in the parish of High Hoyland, in the County of Yorkshire, England, and in proof of this assertion, we find that the dates, family names, marriages and coat of arms are the same. This similarity of names covers over eight hundred years and part of that time on both sides of the Atlantic Ocean. But LeNeve in his "Knights of England," pp. 186-7, appears to have settled this question as he has placed Thomas Clayton, son of John Clayton, of Clayton Hall in Yorkshire, as being born at Clayton Hall in Lancashire. And there is another reason why it is probable that Thomas Clayton was born in Lancashire, namely: His uncle, Thomas Clayton, who was the oldest son and heir and successor to the estates in Lancashire did not marry until 1563, and it is more than probable that the younger brother, having married early, lived at the family mansion until after his children were born.

John Clayton, of Clayton Hall in High Hoyland Parish, County of Yorkshire, was living about 1550. He had two sons, Thomas and Richard. Richard of Wakefield married Joan, daughter of Henry Bentley, by whom he had one son, Daniel of Wakefield. Daniel married (1) Dorothy, daughter of Thomas Methwold, Esq., and had issue Richard, D. D., Master of University College; (2) Jane, daughter of Thomas Leghe, by whom he had four sons: Thomas, Robert, Ferdinando and John.

Thomas Clayton, the eldest son of John Clayton of Clayton Hall, Lancashire (*), married Anguis, daughter of John Thornhill of Fixby, County York, and died about the year 1585, having had issue two sons:

(1) John Clayton of Clayton Hall, who died in 1618. His will is dated the 13th day of April, 1618. He married a daughter of . . . . . Barnby, of Barnby Hall, and had one son, Thomas, of Clayton Hall, who married Alice, daughter of . . . Burdette of Dunly, and sold Clayton Hall to Sir George Cook of Wheatly. This "John" is called Richard in some of the works, but it must be a mistake.

William Clayton, of Oakenshaw, County York, and of the Inner Temple, Barrister at Law, married Margaret, daughter of Jasper Cholmley of East Riding, and died 1627, having had issue eight sons and three daughters.

*See LeNeve's Knights, pp. 186-7.

BIRTHPLACE OF JOHN M. CLAYTON.

DAGSBORO, DELAWARE.

(1) John Clayton, Esq., of the Inner Temple, Barrister at Law in 1626, born April 15, 1592, died April, 1671. He married and had issue (1) John Clayton, of the Inner Temple and a Barrister at Law, born 1620; (2) James Clayton, born 1624. John, the eldest son d. s. p., and James, the second son, became a D. D., and the issue of that branch of the family produced many ministers and lawyers.

2. William, the second son of William Clayton of Oakenshaw, has no record.

3. Thomas, the third son, settled in the City of London, and had issue five sons and two daughters.

4. Sir Jasper Clayton married Mary Thompson. He was an alderman of London and knighted at Guild Hall, July 5, 1660. He married at St. Faith's, London, May 1, 1624, Mary, daughter of William Thompson of Timouth Castle, Northumberland. The "issue of this family was as follows: (1) "Sir John, of London and Parson's Green, Fulham, "Middlesex, admitted to Inner Temple, July 22, 1650, "knighted 1664; married Alice, daughter of Sir William "North Crey, Esq.; (2) George, of London, haberdasher, "born in St. Edmunds, Lombard street, December 24, 1639; "was at Merchant Taylor's School, married Hester, "daughter of Sir Thomas, and sister of Sir Henry "Palmer, of Wingham, Kent, Baronets; (3) Mary, mar- "ried Peter Nourse, of Woodeaton, Oxfordshire; (4) "Prudence; (5) Rebecca married Robert Paston, Earl of "Yarmouth."

George and Hester (Palmer) Clayton had issue: (1) Jasper Clayton, admitted to the Inner Temple, July 12, 1682. He was probably the Jasper Clayton, born July,

1665, who was a scholar of Merchant Taylor's School; (2) George.

"Sir John and Alice (Bowyer) Clayton had issue: "(1) John, born 1665, died November 18, 1737, studied at "one of the universities (probably Cambridge) and was "admitted to the Inner Temple, June 6, 1682; was called "to the bar, and coming to Virginia in 1705, was appointed "Attorney-General of the Colony in 1714 and held the "office until his death. He was also judge of the Court "of Admiralty, frequently a member of the House of "Burgesses, presiding justice of James City County and "Recorder of Williamsburg. One of his descendants has "a large volume containing copies of many of his letters to "his English correspondents. These relate chiefly to the "business affairs of himself and his clients, but some notices "of the family can be gathered from it. It appears that "he owned an estate called Hawkhurst, four miles from "Cranbrooke, Kent, England, which he inherited at his "mother's death (and which descended to his son, John). "There are letters to 'my cousin,' Cecil Bowyer, Esq., of "Denham, which contain messages to Mr. Bowyer's wife, "to 'my uncle' and to 'my Lady Bowyer.' There is "frequent reference to his brother, General Jasper Clayton. "He sends his customary annual present of a box of tobacco "to his steward at Hawkhurst, orders plate with his arms "on it, and frames for two portraits, gives directions in "regard to his son, Thomas, while at Cambridge, and a "medical student in London, acknowledges a present of "'arrack' from London 'which was last night drunk by "some of the best company in Virginia,' refuses and returns "a present of a very costly wig from an English client

"because he makes a rule only to receive his fees as a law-
"yer, and seems to have a very large practice."

"The name of his wife is not known: (2) Jasper, of "Fernhill, in County Bucks, was colonel of the 4th Regi-"ment of Foot, Lieutenant-Governor of Gibraltar, and a "Lieutenant-General in the British Army. He was killed "at the battle of Dettingen in 1743, and buried at Wing-"field, County Bucks.

"The following is an abstract of his will dated March 23, "1742, and proved in London, July 1743, by his son, "Jasper: 'In the name of God, Amen. I, Jasper Clayton, "of Fernhill, in county Bucks, Esq., Lieutenant General of "his Majesties Forces, declare this my last will and testa-"ment. I give to my dearly beloved daughter, Charlotte "Clayton, £3,500 over and above any other sum or sums "of money which her late mother Juliana or myself at any "time have given her. To her, my said daughter, Charlotte "Clayton, the whole and entire furniture of her room at "my house at Fernhill. To my dearly beloved second son, "John Clayton, £2,500. To my son-in-law, Colonel John "Laforey, £100 for family mourning. I give and bequeath "to my very undutiful and lost daughter, Juliana, the "reputed wife of Peter Hooper, who was my servant, "1 shilling and no more. I give to Mrs. Hill, sister to the "late Lady Marsham, £100 to buy her a ring. To my "eldest son, Jasper Clayton, his heirs and assigns forever, "all my capital, messuage and lands at Fernhill, in the "Parish of Wingfield, Bucks, and I recommend him to sell "the same. As to my burial, I desire it may be in the most "frugal manner and most private, thinking everything "otherwise vanity and ostentation. To the Right Hon.

"Samuel, Lord Marsham, one of my executors, £100 "to buy a ring. My eldest son, Jasper Clayton, Lord "Marsham, and said daughter, Charlotte Clayton, executors "and executrix. Dated 23rd March, 1742."

"Not long after the death of General Clayton, his nephew, "John Clayton, of Virginia, writes to his London merchant "(letter book referred to above) that he has shipped to him "a portrait of the late Attorney-General, John Clayton, "which he desired to be sent to 'Mrs. Charlotte Clayton, "Fernhill,' 3, Alice; 4, Mary; 5, Elizabeth. One of these "daughters married John, Lord Lovelace, and another, "Thomas Strickland."

William Clayton, of Oakenshaw, in addition to the above-named, left four other sons: 5, Edward; 6, Daniel, of Norwich, clerk; 7, George, slain at Bois-leduc, and 8, Nathaniel, of London.

THE VIRGINIA BRANCH OF THE CLAYTON FAMILY.

John Clayton, Attorney-General of Virginia, married . . . ., and had issue (1) John Clayton, born at Fulham, England, 1685, and died in Gloucester County, Virginia, 1773. He came to Virginia in 1705, was an eminent botanist, a physician, a member of some of the most learned societies of Europe, President of the Virginia Society for Promoting Useful Knowledge, 1773; and author of 'Flora Virginica'." "It appears that John Clayton married Jan. 21, 1723, Elizabeth Whiting of Gloucester County. Issue: Several sons and daughters. The eldest son was named John, another named Jasper. He was clerk of the Gloucester Committee of Safety,

JOSHUA CLAYTON, M. D.
GOVERNOR OF DELAWARE.
U. S. SENATOR.

1774-5. He served in the cavalry of the Revolutionary Army and married Courtney, daughter of General John Baylor of New Market, Caroline, and had issue (1) Baylor; (2) Arthur B., born 1800, in Gloucester County, and died March 31, 1845; (3) Caroline, (4) Courtney. A branch of this family was resident in New Kent, descendants of Attorney-General John Clayton. Colonel William Clayton of New Kent, a grandson of Attorney-General John Clayton, was a member of the House of Burgesses, from New Kent from 1769 (and perhaps earlier) to 1774; of the Convention of 1776; of the House of Delegates of 1776 and other years, and the Convention of 1788. Of the same branch was Colonel Wm. Beverly Clayton, clerk of New Kent, 1787 to 1803 and later. Other members of the family were Jasper Clayton, who married a daughter of Edmund Berkeley of Barn Elms, Middlesex County.

Arthur Clayton was a member of the House of Delegates from Louisa from 1817-1818. Jasper S. Clayton was appointed Justice of Matthews in 1791, and James and Joseph Clayton were living in Gloucester in 1840.

From these references it appears that John Clayton, the Attorney-General, had at least three sons, John, Thomas and Arthur, and in all probability a son named Samuel, for it appears by Slaughter's History of Culpepper County, that Samuel Clayton, of New Kent, who is supposed to be a son of John Clayton, the Attorney-General of Virginia, married Elizabeth Pendleton, a daughter of Philip Pendleton, and as he is the first by that name he will be called Philip Clayton (1). He married Anne Coleman. They had a son, Samuel Clayton, who married his cousin, Anne

Coleman, and among their children was Major Philip Clayton II, an officer in the Revolutionary Army. Philip Clayton I was the grandfather of Captain Philip Slaughter, another officer in the Revolutionary Army. He lived at "Catalpa," Virginia.

Philip Clayton II married Mildred Dixon and moved from Virginia to Georgia. One of their sons was named Augustin Smith Clayton. He was born in Petersburg, Va., November 27, 1783. In 1784 his family moved to Richmond County, Ga. In February, 1790, on the occasion of the visit of President Washington to Augusta, Ga., Augustin Smith Clayton, the 7-year old boy was selected to make a speech of welcome to the President, which so pleased Washington that he presented the boy with a copy of "Salust" duly inscribed. "He graduated at Franklin College, was distinguished at the bar, was a judge of the Western Circuit and a member of Congress, where he won a national reputation." He was an able statesman, jurist, and man of letters, and left his impress upon the policy and literature of the State. He married Julia Carnes, by whom he had nine children, among them Philip, born at Athens, Ga., March 19, 1815. He died June 1, 1839, in the 56th year of his age.

Home of Gov. Joshua Clayton.

THE PENNSYLVANIA BRANCH OF THE CLAYTON FAMILY.

William Clayton, one of the sons of Thomas Clayton of London, and a grandson of William Clayton of Oakenshaw of County Yorkshire, England, had a patent granted to him by the British government for five hundred acres of land at Chichester, Pa., where he settled in 1671, and on the 13th day of September, 1681, he presided over the first court held under the proprietory government at Upland in Chester county, Pennsylvania. His son, William Clayton, Jr., was one of the jurors of that court. William Clayton, (1) was a member of Penn's Council during 1683-1684, and assisted in drafting most of the laws for Pennsylvania at that time. He was a personal friend of William Penn. He was a cousin of Joshua Clayton, who settled in Delaware, and was the ancestor of the numerous Claytons who have been prominent in Pennsylvania, and, after a busy life, died about 1691.

He was a man of prominence among the Quakers and in the active part which he took in the government at that time. It appears that a company of land owners in New Jersey had sent him over to this country to look after their interests and after attending to those duties, he settled in Chichester, Pennsylvania.

"William Clayton (1) of Chichester, Pa., was the son of "Thomas Clayton, a third son of William Clayton, of Okenshaw, and a brother of Sir Jasper Clayton of London, and "a grandson of Thomas Clayton of Clayton Hall, in York-"shire." Note.—See Rambles and Reflections of Hon.

T. J. Clayton, p. 297. "The first son of Thomas Clayton, "of Clayton Hall, died a minor. His second son was "William of Okenshaw. He was known as a barrister of "the Inner Temple. He died in 1627. The estate known "as 'Clayton Hall' descended to Thomas Clayton (2), who "was in possession as heir in 1666. He had a son, William, "who came to this country in 1671, and is the ancestor of "our family, and will be hereafter called 'William of "Chichester.' * * * * * * Thomas (2) also had "a son John, who was a barrister of the Inner Temple. He "died April 6, 1666." After William Clayton settled in Chichester, Pennsylvania, his cousin, Joshua Clayton, another grand-son of William Clayton of Okenshaw, accompanied William Penn to this country on his first visit. He had two sons John and Joshua who settled in Little Creek Hundred, Kent County in the State of Delaware, who became the ancestors of that branch of the Clayton family.

William Clayton, with his family, arrived in the ship "Kent" from London in company with certain commissioners sent out by the proprietors of New Jersey to purchase lands from the Indians. He left many prominent descendants and his branch of the family occupies prominent positions in Pennsylvania, Arkansas, Texas, Colorado, Illinois and many other states. The late Hon. Thomas J. Clayton, President Judge of Delaware County who was admitted to the bar in 1850, and died in 1900, Hon. Powell Clayton of Arkansas, now Ambassador to Mexico, the late Henry Armitt Brown a distinguished lawyer and orator of Philadelphia are lineal descendants of William Clayton of Chichester. William Clayton of Chichester was nearly related to Hon. John Clayton, Attorney General of Virginia.

He was a personal friend of William Penn, and it is known that Penn selected a majority of his councilors from among his relatives or personal friends, in order that he might have a majority of the council. To illustrate the language used in 1681, the following quotations from Cope's History of Chester County Pennsylvania pp. 18-19 is given.

"Province of Pennsylvania; at the Cort at Vpland,
"September 13, 1681—

"Mr. William Clayton,	Mr. Rober Lucas,
"Mr. William Warner,	Mr. Lassey Cock,
"Mr. Robert Wade,	Mr. Swan Swanson,
"Mr. Otto Ernst Cock,	Mr. Andreas Bankson,
"Mr. William Byles,	*Justices present.*

"Mr. John Test, *Sheriffe.*
"Mr. Tho. Revell, *Clerke.*"

"Of the justices, five are Englishmen, four Swedes, two "of whom had been members of the former court.

"The jurors in attendance appeared to have been twenty-six."

THE DELAWARE BRANCH OF THE CLAYTON FAMILY.

In order that this sketch of the "Clayton Family" may be understood, it is given in genealogical order for six generations by numbers after each individual name, but as certain prominent members of the family have an historical interest, their history is intended to precede the table using the numbers there given.

Joshua Clayton (1) is spoken of by some of the authorities as a minister of the Gospel and that he visited or settled finally in Virginia. It will be found that there was a

Thomas Clayton in Virginia on York River who was a prominent lawyer as early as 1680, who had a large practice from London merchants. Among the archives of Pennsylvania it appears that on the 25th of October, 1682 Thomas Clayton took up land in Chester County, Pennsylvania. It must be remembered that Sir John Clayton of London was a first cousin of Joshua Clayton (1) and that his son John settled in Virginia; and as Virginia and the three Delaware Counties, which were parts of Pennsylvania, were in close proximity, it required but little time to complete a trip to and from each state. There appear to be no records in the State of Delaware showing any will or letters of administration on the estate of Joshua Clayton (1). It is claimed that he came to this country with William Penn on his first visit. It has been handed down from generation to generation both in Delaware and Pennsylvania that William Clayton (1) of Pennsylvania, and Joshua Clayton (1) of Delaware were cousins. The late Hon. John M. Clayton while Secretary of State under President Taylor, conversed with the Virginia branch of the Clayton Family on the subject of the relationship between the two families, and after going over all the facts they decided that the Virginia Claytons and the Delaware Claytons were from the same original stock.

The late Judge Clayton of Pennsylvania states in his biography of the family that William Clayton (1) and Joshua Clayton (1) were descendants of Thomas Clayton of Clayton Hall in the parish of Highhoyland County York, England.

Joshua Clayton (1) married * * * * * * * by whom he had issue, two sons, John (2) and Joshua (3,) both of whom settled in Kent County, Delaware, perhaps as early as 1695.

John Clayton and Joshua Clayton must have been very old men at the time of their respective deaths, which happened in 1759 and 1761. From these two men, the record of the "Clayton Family" is verified by wills, deeds, bibles, Friends' Yearly Meeting Records, tombstones and family history. John and Joshua Clayton must have been born about 1675 or 1677, as they purchased lands jointly in Kent County, Delaware as early as 1698. See Deed Book "C", Volume I, page 211 etc. John Clayton (2) son of Joshua (1) of whom hereafter. Joshua Clayton (3) son of Joshua Clayton (1) and brother of John Clayton (2) settled in Little Creek Hundred, Kent County, Delaware, and became a prominent member of the Society of Friends, and he appears to have taken a very decided and active part in all their meetings from 1716 to the date of his death in January 1761.

He became a large land owner in Kent County, was a very religious and devoted Quaker, and lived on his home plantation at the time of his death. He married * * * * * * * by whom he had three daughters: Lydia (6) who married John Cowgill on the 16th day of December 1720, Sarah, (7) who married Thomas Cowgill, Elizabeth (8) who married Mark Manlove, Jr., on the 19th day of August 1730.

Joshua Clayton (3) died about the first day of January A. D. 1761, having made his last will and testament dated the 2nd day of September A. D. 1760, probated at Dover, Delaware on the sixth day of January A. D. 1761, and registered in Will Book "K" page 225 etc., wherein he devised as follows:—ITEM: "I leave unto my grand-

"daughter Eunice Osbourne, (wife of Jonathon Osbourne) "my now dwelling plantation, being part of a tract of land "called 'Higham's Ferry,' and a part of a tract of land "called 'Wilton Creek.'" He also left other lands and a number of slaves to his grand-children and the following grand-children are named as devisees:—John Cowgill, Clayton Cowgill, Ezekiel Cowgill, Thomas Cowgill, Sarah Register, who was the wife of John Register of Talbot County, Md., Elizabeth Neal, Jean Smith, Lydia Durborough and the said Eunice Osbourne.

John Clayton (2) married Grace * * * by whom he had issue two sons and one daughter, to wit: John Clayton (4) James Clayton (5) and * * * Clayton (5½) who married * * * Caldwell by whom she had a son John Caldwell and a daughter Sarah Caldwell.

John Clayton (4) was a prominent man in the County, a large land owner and died in 1758 having made his last will and Testament dated the 4th day of December A. D. 1754, probated at Dover on the 9th day of May A. D. 1759 and recorded in Will Book K. page 203, etc, wherein he constituted and appointed his son James (5) his Executor and devised his estate to his two grand-children John Caldwell and Sarah Caldwell, his two sons John Clayton (4) and James Clayton (5) and his widow Grace Clayton.

John Clayton, Jr. (4) a son of John and Grace Clayton, was returned High Sheriff of Kent County Delaware, in 1752-1753, and was styled John Clayton, Jr. He was also a Lieutenant and (perhaps a Captain) in the Continental Army in 1757, and his name appears in a Caveat in the land office in 1760, he also appears as the Administrator of the Estate of his brother James in 1761. He appears to have

RACHEL McCLEARY CLAYTON,
THE WIFE OF GOVERNOR JOSHUA CLAYTON
AND HER TWO SONS.

JAMES LAWSON CLAYTON.

RICHARD CLAYTON.

been the first Clayton to hold public office in the State of Delaware and left an only son who d. s. p.

John Clayton (11) a son of James (5) and Grace Clayton, b. 1749, and d., 1802. m. Mary Mason Manlove by whom he had two sons.

His will is dated April 1, 1794, probated at Dover in Will Book O, page 67, etc., wherein he provided that in the event of the death of his two sons James and Edward Clayton in their minority, his estate should be divided between James Lawson Clayton, Richard Clayton and Thomas Clayton, sons of his brother Dr. Joshua Clayton, to John Clayton and Charles Clayton, sons of his brother Thomas Clayton—and James Hanson, a son of his sister Lydia Hanson, (nee Clayton).

He was appointed a Judge in Admiralty under the Constitution of 1776, and also appointed fourth Justice of the Court of C. P. for Kent County, Delaware on the 15th day of February 1788, and again appointed third Justice of the same Court on the 8th day of February 1790. About 1792, he was High Sheriff of Kent County, Delaware, and while acting in that capacity, compelled the Legislature of the State, then in session, (May 1792) to vacate the Court House, and they adjourned to Duck Creek, Cross Roads, (now Smyrna).

This act showed the strong character of the man. He took a deep interest in Colonial politics, in the Revolution, and in the Government afterwards. He was appointed one of the Associate Judges of the Court of C. P. of the State of Delaware on the 16th day of September A. D. 1793, which position he occupied until the time of his death 1802. He was a large land owner in Kent County, Delaware and resided in Murderkill Hundred. He left two sons, James and Edward Manlove, whose descendants largely live in the Southern States, none in Delaware.

The portrait of Judge John Clayton appearing in this sketch was made from a miniature painted in Philadelphia in 1784, and now in the possession of the family.

IV. Joshua Clayton (10) born in 1744, married Mrs. Rachel McCleary an adopted daughter of Richard Bassett, an early Governor of the State of Delaware. Joshua Clayton was a practicing physician and was a surgeon in the Revolutionary Army. He was elected Major of the Bohemia Batallion on the 6th day of January, 1776, and was commissioned Colonel by General Washington just before the battle of Brandywine; it is said that General Washington placed him on his staff "in order to make a good appear-"ance when receiving the sword of General Howe, whom "he expected to take at that place."

Colonel Dr. Joshua Clayton held many prominent positions in the army, state and nation. He was the last President of the State of Delaware, and the first governor under the new Constitution, and in 1798 was elected to the United States Senate. He filled each and every position with honor to himself, his state and the nation. He was largely interested in the ownership of Bohemia Manor, and he and Richard Bassett owned nearly all of that ancient manor of 20,000 acres of land lying in New Castle County, Delaware and Cecil County, Maryland. He took the yellow fever in 1798, and against the entreaties of Dr. Rush, returned to his home in Bohemia Manor, where he died leaving to survive him three sons:—James Lawson (16,) Richard (17,) Thomas (18).

PROFILE SILHOUETTE OF JOHN M. CLAYTON.

Thomas Clayton (18) was born at Massey's Cross Roads, Maryland in July 1777. He married Jennette Macomb, daughter of Eleazer Macomb, studied law, and was admitted to the Delaware Bar in 1799. He practiced law at Dover and was appointed Secretary of State in 1808, Attorney General in 1811, elected to the Congress in 1814, and took his seat in the Senate of the United States January 15, 1824 to fill the unexpired term of Hon. Cæsar A. Rodney. In 1828 he was appointed Chief Justice of the State of Delaware. He was again elected to the United States Senate in 1841 and at the expiration of his term retired to private life at New Castle where he died August 31, 1854, having had issue an only son and two daughters:—Joshua Clayton (39) b August 2, 1802, Elizabeth (40,) Jennette (41).

JOHN M. CLAYTON.

John M. Clayton, (25) the son of James Clayton (15) and Sarah (Middleton) Clayton his wife was born at Dagsboro, Sussex County, Delaware, November 24th, 1796. After a preliminary education at Lewes he graduated from Yale College and studied law with his cousin, Hon. Thomas Clayton, afterwards Chief Justice of the State. He was admitted to the Delaware bar in 1819, and soon showed a bent toward politics, serving as Secretary of State from 1826 to 1828. As the leader of the Adams party in 1828 he carried the state and was rewarded by election to the United States Senate entering that body at the early age of thirty-two. He served as a Senator with Webster, Clay, Calhoun and Benton and soon became a prominent figure in National Politics. Was re-elected to the Senate in 1835, and was twice after elected in 1845 and in 1853. During Zachary Taylor's brief term as President he served as Secretary of State and negotiated the celebrated Clayton-Bulwer treaty. For three years he occupied the office of Chief Justice of the State.

He was a born leader of men. No man whom Delaware has produced has measured higher in intellectual capacity or in combination of rare gifts. As a man he was tender and true, as a lawyer and judge he occupied the highest rank, and as an advocate and statesman none surpassed him. His life was full of accomplishments and at his death on November 9th, 1856 his remains were laid at rest in the graveyard of the Presbyterian Church at Dover.

Joshua Clayton, son of Thomas and Emma (Purner) Clayton was born February 8th, 1871. He was the grandson of Colonel Joshua the great grandson of Chief Justice Thomas, and great-great grandson of Governor Joshua. After being educated at the Middletown Academy he studied law with Albert Constable, Esq., at Elkton, Maryland, and was admitted to the Cecil County bar in 1899, and was a member of the Maryland House of Delegates in 1901. Mr. Clayton is an active man with much of the ability, that has made the Clayton family famous, and as a lawyer promises to make a successful career.

GENEALOGICAL TABLE, FOR SIX GENERATIONS, OF THE DELAWARE FAMILY OF CLAYTONS.

FIRST GENERATION:—

Children of Joshua Clayton (1), first settler in Delaware:

John (2) d 1758 m Grace . . . . . .

Joshua (3) a Quaker preacher d 1760.

SECOND GENERATION.

Children of John Clayton (2) and Grace his wife:

John (4)

James (5) m Grace . . . . . . d about May 10, 1761.

Children of Joshua Clayton (3) and . . . . . his wife:—

Lydia (6) m John Cowgill 12-16-1720,

Sarah (7) m Thomas Cowgill,

Elizabeth (8) m Mark Manlove, Jr., 8-19-1730.

THIRD GENERATION.

Children of John Clayton (4):

John Edmund (9) d. s. p.

Children of James Clayton (5) and Grace . . . his wife:

Joshua (10) b 1744, d 1798, m Rachel McCleary.

John (11) b 1749, d 1802 m Mary Mason Manlove.

James (12) d in infancy.

Thomas (13) d 1785 m Elizabeth Wharton of Philadelphia.

Lydia (14) m Joseph Hanson by whom she had one son John.

Grace (14¼) b . . . . d.

Miriam (14½).

Amelia (14¾).

George b 3-24-1761 renamed James (15) d 11-24-1820, m Sarah Middleton 8-18-1791, a daughter of Ignatius Middleton of Annapolis, Md.

FOURTH GENERATION.

Children of Joshua Clayton (10) and Rachael McCleary his wife:

James Lawson (16) b 7-14-1769, d 3-19-1833 m Elizabeth Polk 12-16-1795.

Richard (17) b 1774, d 1836, m first, Mary Richardson, second Mary Lawrenson, third Araminta Lewis.

Thomas (18), b 7- 1777, d 8-21-1854, m Jennette Macomb.

Children of John Clayton (11) and Mary Manlove, his wife:

James (19) b. 1780, d 1825, m Sarah Medford.

Edward Manlove (20) d 1819, m Rachel H. Manlove 11-20-1811.

Children of Thomas Clayton (13) and Elizabeth Wharton his wife:

Charles (21) d. s. p.

John (22) d. s. p.

Children of Pearse Clayton (14) and . . . . Hanson her husband:

James (23).

Children of James Clayton (15) and Sarah Middleton his wife:

Lydia (24) b. 9-18-1794, m John Kellam of Accomac County, Virginia and d. s. p.

John Middleton (25) b 11-24-1796 m Sallie Ann Fisher daughter of Dr. James Fisher, 9-12-1822 at Middletown, Del. by the Rev. (afterward Dr.) Samuel Brinckle and d 11-9-1856.

Harriet M. (26) b 5-8-1798 m Walter Douglass 10-6-1814 who d 4-20-1826. She married secondly Henry W. Peterson of Canada.

Judge John Clayton.
1749-1802.

Henry (27) b 3-2-1800 d 6-17-1800.

Elizabeth (28) b 9-12-1801 d. s. p. 3-5-1822.

Mary Ann (29) b 12-8-1803 m George T. Fisher.

James Henry (30) b 9-12-1809 d. s. p. 6-7-1836.

FIFTH GENERATION.

Children of James Lawson Clayton (16) and Elizabeth Polk, his wife:

Rachel (31), born 1797, d 1890, m Nathaniel Smithers, d. s. p.

John L. (32) b 1788 d m Ellen M. Clark.

Margaret (33) b 1799 died in infancy.

Hester (34) b 1802 died in infancy.

Amelia (35) b 1803 d 1891 m Thomas C. Hambley.

Anna (36), b 1805, d 1891, m Joshua Clayton (42).

Susanna (37) b 1808 died in infancy.

James (38) b 1810 died in infancy.

Children of Richard Clayton (17) and Mary Richardson his first wife.

Joshua (42) b 1794, d 1854, m Anna White Clayton (36).

James (43) b 1803 d 1857 m Emeline Lewis.

Thomas E. (44) b 1800 d 1858 m Sarah Lawrenson.

Mary (45) b 1797 d 1845 m first, Richard Lawrenson, secondly, George Lewis.

Children of Richard Clayton (17) and Mary Lawrenson, his second wife.

Richard T. P. (46), b 1808, m Ann Templeton.

Jennette (47), died unmarried.

Children of Richard Clayton (17) and Araminta Lewis his third wife:

Lydia A. (48) b 1816 d 1849 m Joshua Clayton (39).

Children of Thomas Clayton (18) and Jennette Macomb his wife:

Joshua (39) b 1802 d 1888, m first, Lydia A. Clayton m secondly, Martha E. Lockwood.

Elizabeth (40) b 1804 d 1847 m Nathaniel Young.

Jennette (41) b 1805 d 1848 m Robert Frame.

Children of James Clayton (17) and Sarah Medford his wife:

Henry M. (49) b 12-31-1810 d 11-13-1888 m Mary E. Woodland.

John (50) b 1819 d 3-14-1881 m Anna B. Colton.

Susan M. (51) b 7-23-1802 d 8-6-1881 d. s. p.

Mary A. (52) b 7-17-1804 d 11-17-1881 d. s. p.

Children of Edward Manlove Clayton (20) and Rachel H. Manlove his wife:

Ann Rebecca (53) b 8-21-1812 d 3-31-1883 m James W. Dunklin.

Elizabeth W. (54) b 10-24-1815 d 12-1-1898 m Charles E. Lavender.

Mary Louisa (55) b 4-21-1817 unmarried.

Children of John M. Clayton (25) and Sarah Middleton his wife:

James Fisher (56), unmarried, b 7-11-1823, d. s. p. 3-1-1851.

Charles McClymont (57) b 2-3-1835, d. s. p. 7-20-1849.

Children of Harriet M. Clayton (26) and Walter Douglas her husband.

Margaret A. (58) b 4-17-1816 m Joseph P. Comegys 3-30-1837.

James Clayton (59) b 11-24-1817 m Ellen Stewart Sinclair 11-7-1848.

Children of Mary Ann Clayton (29) and George T. Fisher her husband.

James C. (60) died unmarried.

John C. (61) died unmarried.

Sixth Generation.

Children of John L. Clayton (32) and Ellen M. Clark, his wife:

Julius (62).

James W. (63).

Theodore (64).

John P. (65).

Henry (66).

Children of Amelia Clayton (35) and Thomas C. Hambley her husband:

Thomas C. Jr. (67) died young.

Henrietta M. (68) m Charles M. Siter.

William T. (69) died 1894.

Samuel C. (70) unmarried.

Children of Anna White Clayton (36) and Joshua Clayton her husband;

Charles, (71) m Emma Clark.

Joshua (73) m Lavinia Moyer.

Children of Joshua Clayton (39) and Lydia A. Clayton his first wife:

Thomas (74) b 12-6-1833 d 9-20-1896.

Henry (75) b 1839 d 1896.

Richard (76) b 1842 d 1898.

Children of Joshua Clayton (39) and Martha E. Lockwood his second wife:

Adalaide Y. (77) m Charles S. Ellison.

Macomb (78) m Elizabeth Porter Laws.

Mary (79) m J. Fletcher Price.

Elizabeth (80) m Dr. Williams.

Joshua (81) m Estelle Pennington.

Frances (82) m Nathaniel J. Williams.

Eugene (83) m Anna J. Wilson.

Children of Elizabeth Clayton (40) and Nathaniel Young her husband:

Jennette (84) unmarried.

Adelaide (85) unmarried.

Children of Jennette Clayton (41) and Robert Frame, her husband:

Robert (86) b 1837 m Hetty McColley d 1902.

Thomas C. (87) b 1840 m Mary Layton.

Julia (88) b 1844 unmarried.

Children of Joshua Clayton (42) and Anna White Clayton (36) his wife:

See ante. No. 36.

Children of James Clayton (43) and Emeline Lewis his wife:

Arianna (89) m Edward Townsend.

George (90) died unmarried.

Caroline (91) m Arthur Johns.

Children of Thomas E. Clayton (44) and Sarah Lawrenson his wife:

Emma Elizabeth (92) m James A. Lewis.

Children of Mary Clayton (45) and Richard Lawrenson her first husband:

Eliza (93) m George Templeman.

Children of Mary Clayton (45) and George Lewis her second husband:

THOMAS CLAYTON.
CHEIF JUSTICE OF DELAWARE.
U. S. SENATOR.

James A. (94) m Emma Elizabeth Clayton (see foot note).

Matilda m Dr. Swartz.

Children of Richard T. P. Clayton (46) . . and his wife:

Richard (95) married,

Anna (96) m James Jamison.

Children of Lydia A. Clayton (48) and Joshua Clayton her husband:

See ante. No. 39.

Children of Henry M. Clayton (49) and Mary E. Woodland his wife:

James W. (97) b 10-30-1837) m Elizabeth Hunter.

Henry M. (98) b 6-9-1844 d 7-3-1901 married first Adelia Tracy secondly Mary Pemberton.

John A. (99) b 1850 d 1899 m Mary . . . . . .

Mary E. (100) b 1838 d 1902 m John Thompson.

Sarah E. (101) b 7-16-1848 m Henry Snow Bartlett.

Children of John Clayton (50) and Anna B. Colton his wife:

Anna B. (102) b 1847 d 1899 m J. G. R. McElroy.

Louisa B. (103) b 1852 m W. H. Gilpin.

Ella M. (104) b 1858 d 1901 unmarried.

Children of Ann Rebecca Clayton (53) and James W. Dunklin her husband:

Edward C. (105) b 6-23-1832 d 1-11-1900.

Mary E. (106) b 1-10-1835 d 1-20-1902.

William H. (107) b 3-6-1837 d 5-7-1864.

Virgie J. (108) b 9-26-1841 d 1-14-1885.

Florence E. (109) b 10-16-1845.

Charles P. (110) b 11-18-1847.

NOTE—This James A. Lewis (the son of a Clayton woman) was the only relative of John M. Clayton ever appointed to office by him, he being his private secretary, and the man who prepared the rough draft of the Clayton-Bulwer Treaty.

Children of Elizabeth W. Clayton (54) and Charles E. Lavender her husband:

Mary Louisa (111) b 5-2-1837.

Edward C. (112) b 5-13-1839 d 6-1-1892.

Della (113) b 6-15-1842 d 10-23-1865.

Charles H. (114) b 11-16-1843.

Children of Margaret A. Douglass (58) and Joseph P. Comegys her husband:

Walter Douglass (115) b 9-12-1838 m 12-29-1863 Anna L. Bell dau of Hon. John Bell of Tennessee, issue one child which died in infancy.

Walter Douglas Comegys (116) d. s. p. 11-28-1877.

Harriet Clayton (117) b 9-26-1840, living.

Cornelia (118) b . . . . d.s. p. 9-25-1878.

Children of James Clayton Douglas (59) and Ella Stewart Sinclair his wife:

Constance Margaret (119) b 3-20-1852 m 1-16-1884 Francis N. Buck.

Clayton Douglas (120) b 3-27-1854 d. s. p. 2-21-1872.

EXTRACT FROM THE FAMILY BIBLE OF THE LATE HON. JOHN M. CLAYTON.

" My father gave me the following pedigree of the Clayton " family. Joshua Clayton came to America from England " with William Penn. He left sons *John* and Joshua. " Joshua left one daughter, who married a Cowgill, and the " Cowgill family in Delaware is connected with mine, being " the descendants of that daughter. John left sons *James* " and John. James left sons Joshua, John, Thomas, James " and George. John (Senior of John) left a son John " Edmunds Clayton who died without issue. Joshua (of

"James) left Thomas, James, Richard and Thomas. John "(of James) left James and Edward now dead.

"Thomas (of James) died leaving two sons John and "Charles who died without issue.

"James died an infant a few days after his father and "then George was renamed James after his father. He was "born March 24, 1761, married my mother August 18, "1791 and left at his death on the 24th day of November "1820 Lydia, wife of John Kellam, John M. Clayton, "Harriet, wife of Walter Douglass, Elizabeth Clayton, "Mary Ann, wife of G. T. Fisher, and James H. M. Clayton.

Attest:

[Signed] JOHN M. CLAYTON."

GENERAL COMMENT.

It will be found by an examination of the admission of the great number of lawyers produced by the Clayton family; that for over three hundred years either in this country or England, some of them have graced the bar. We will begin with 1590 when William Clayton of Okenshaw County, York, England, of the Inner Temple Barrister at law had been admitted, and dying in 1627 left a son John Clayton of the Inner Temple, Barrister at Law, admitted in 1626, who died in 1671, leaving a son John Clayton of the Inner Temple, Barrister at Law, who died subsequent to 1705.

From 1705 to 1743 John Clayton, a son of Rev. James Clayton, and great grand-son of William Clayton, of Okenshaw, was a member of the Middle Temple.

From 1650 to 1682 Sir John Clayton, a son of Sir Jasper Clayton;

From 1682 to 1737 John Clayton of Va., a son of Sir John Clayton;

From 1727 to 1772 Richard Clayton, Lord Chief Justice of Ireland;

From 1762 to 1824 Sir Richard Clayton, Baronet.

From 1799 to 1854 Thomas Clayton, late Chief Justice of Delaware;

From 1819 to 1856 John M. Clayton also late Chief Justice of Delaware;

From 1825 to 1888 Joshua Clayton of Delaware;

1850 to 1900 Thomas J. Clayton, late Judge of Delaware County, Pennsylvania;

From 1899 to 1904 Joshua Clayton of Maryland who is now living.

This family has not been any less conspicuous in its number of physicians. From 1705 to 1773 John Clayton was a physician in Gloucester County, Virginia. From about 1770 to 1798 Dr. Joshua Clayton was a physician in Delaware, and from the year 1800 to the present time there have been so many physicians from this family it would take a book to contain their names. They are scattered all over the United States. We find the ministry beginning about 1100 and continuing until the present day.

The ministers of the Gospel in this family represented the Roman Catholic, Protestant Episcopal, Presbyterian, Methodist and other denominations. Many of them became Quakers during the Seventeenth century. From this array of talented men one might expect to find a man filling the highest station in life, one who would be singled out among men as a great leader, lawyer, orator and statesman, and it was left to the Diamond State to produce such a man.

We can name with praise our own John M. Clayton as the man of great natural abilities, well cultivated and thoroughly matured. Here we find the greatest of great lawyers, the brighest of brilliant orators, the profoundest of jurists, the most astute of astute statesmen, and one of the deepest, clearest and strongest diplomats. He honored the name of "Clayton," the name of the State of Delaware and the nation that gave him place and position. He was the boy orator of the state that loved him and his name will go down in history as the one man who could fill the highest judicial chair of his state, who could challenge the greatest statesmen to combat and meet the diplomats of the world with such marked ability that they all honored him. Well may the state be proud of her noble statesman. One word more and we will close and that is to appeal to you all to uphold the honor of this state with such men in the halls of our national legislature. For further information on John M. Clayton see Memoir of his life, containing over 300 pages by the late Hon. Joseph P. Comegys, Chief Justice of the State of Delaware, and a former student in his office.

ABBREVIATIONS.

b. born; s. succeeded; d. died; d. s. p. died without issue; m. married; unm. unmarried; dau. daughter.

Books and papers referred to in manuscript.

Playfair's British Family Antiquities Vol. VII. p. 159 &c.

Dugdale's Visitations of Yorkshire p. 266.

Slaughter's St. Mark's Parish, Culpepper Co., Va. pp. 125-126-127.

Rambles and Reflections of T. J. Clayton, late President Judge of Delaware County, Pa., pp. 396-7-8-9 &c.

Burk's Landed Gentry of England, Vol. I. p. 360.

History of Chester County, Pa., by Gilbert Cope.

Lamb's Biographical Dictionary. Sir Peter Leycester's Antiquities.

Letters of Rev. John Clayton of Crofton, Wakefield Co., York, England.

May 12, 1688, "Account of Va." published in Miscellanea Curiosa, Vol. III. pp. 281-293-301-312-327 &c. Historical Society of Virginia.

Scharf's History of Delaware, Vol. I. and II.

Quaker Record of Births, marriages and deaths of Delaware families.

Chalmer's Historical Dictionary, Vol. IX. p. 435.

Testa de Nevil a Survey of England, A. D. 1247 pp. 372-396-397-403.

Baines Lancashire and Cheshire "Past and Present" Vol. I. Division II. pp. 531-530-602-603. Delaware Court Records.

Pennsylvania Archives, Vol. I.

Personal Reminiscenses of members of the Clayton family, and special mention is made of Hon. Thomas J. Clayton, Dr. Thomas Clayton Frame, Dr. Joshua Clayton of Philadelphia, Joshua Clayton, Esq., of Elkton, Md., H. C. Conrad, Esq., and Miss Harriet Clayton Comegys.